Greater Than a Tourist Book Series Reviews from Readers

I think the series is wonderful and beneficial for tourists to get information before visiting the city.

-Seckin Zumbul, Izmir Turkey

I am a world traveler who has read many trip guides but this one really made a difference for me. I would call it a heartfelt creation of a local guide expert instead of just a guide.

-Susy, Isla Holbox, Mexico

New to the area like me, this is a must have!

-Joe, Bloomington, USA

This is a good series that gets down to it when looking for things to do at your destination without having to read a novel for just a few ideas.

-Rachel, Monterey, USA

Good information to have to plan my trip to this destination.

-Pennie Farrell, Mexico

Great ideas for a port day.

-Mary Martin USA

Aptly titled, you won't just be a tourist after reading this book. You'll be greater than a tourist!

-Alan Warner, Grand Rapids, USA

Even though I only have three days to spend in San Miguel in an upcoming visit, I will use the author's suggestions to guide some of my time there. An easy read - with chapters named to guide me in directions I want to go.

-Robert Catapano, USA

Great insights from a local perspective! Useful information and a very good value!

-Sarah, USA

This series provides an in-depth experience through the eyes of a local. Reading these series will help you to travel the city in with confidence and it'll make your journey a unique one.

-Andrew Teoh, Ipoh, Malaysia

GREATER THAN A TOURIST- CHESTER CHESHIRE UNITED KINGDOM

50 Travel Tips from a Local

Leah Fryer

Cover designed by: Ivana Stamenkovic
Cover Image: https://pixabay.com/en/roman-chesters-wall-ruin-castle-199998/

CZYK Publishing Since 2011.

Greater Than a Tourist
Visit our website at www.GreaterThanaTourist.com

Lock Haven, PA

ISBN: 9781791867805

>TOURIST

50 TRAVEL TIPS FROM A LOCAL

BOOK DESCRIPTION

Are you excited about planning your next trip?

Do you want to try something new?

Would you like some guidance from a local?

If you answered yes to any of these questions, then this Greater Than a Tourist book is for you.

Greater Than a Tourist- Chester, Cheshire, United Kingdom by Leah Fryer offers the inside scoop on Chester. Most travel books tell you how to travel like a tourist. Although there is nothing wrong with that, as part of the Greater Than a Tourist series, this book will give you travel tips from someone who has lived at your next travel destination.

In these pages, you will discover advice that will help you throughout your stay. This book will not tell you exact addresses or store hours but instead will give you excitement and knowledge from a local that you may not find in other smaller print travel books.

Travel like a local. Slow down, stay in one place, and get to know the people and the culture. By the time you finish this book, you will be eager and prepared to travel to your next destination.

TABLE OF CONTENTS

15. Try Quid's In
16. Recover From A Night Out With Some Pizza
17. Wash It Down With A Milkshake
18. Have Another Shake
19. Fine Dine A Waffle
20. Enjoy A Crepe Instead
21. Chow Down On A Yorkshire Pudding
22. Go Down To The River
23. Eat At Hickory's
24. Rent A Paddleboat
25. Take A Boat Tour
26. Cross The Bridge
27. Take A Scenic Nature Walk
28. Sip On A Mojito
29. Combine Chemistry And Drinking
30. Try Out Flowers And Tea
31. Try More Flowers And Food
32. Eat At A Tavern
33. Go Indoor Shopping
34. Go Outdoor Shopping
35. Visit The Market
36. Do Some More Shopping
37. Go See A Movie
38. See Some Birds
39. Visit The Zoo
40. Go To The Aquarium

DEDICATION

This book is dedicated to Izey and Sav – my two favorite tourists.

ABOUT THE AUTHOR

Leah Fryer is a third-year senior at Clarion University of Pennsylvania who lives in PA, but is soon moving to Chester. Leah loves to read, write, watch movies, and adventure anywhere possible with her friends.

Leah loves to travel whenever she can. She studied abroad in Chester which gave her the amazing opportunity to live there for five months. After Chester, her favorite place to travel is Paris, but she has also been to other beautiful cities in Europe, as well as all over England. Since leaving Chester, Leah has gone back to England twice and plans to move there after graduation.

HOW TO USE THIS BOOK

The Greater Than a Tourist book series was written by someone who has lived in an area for over three months. The goal of this book is to help travelers either dream or experience different locations by providing opinions from a local. The author has made suggestions based on their own experiences. Please do your own research before traveling to the area in case the suggested places are unavailable.

Travel Advisories: As a first step in planning any trip abroad, check the Travel Advisories for your intended destination.
https://travel.state.gov/content/travel/en/traveladvisories/traveladvisories.html

FROM THE PUBLISHER

Traveling can be one of the most important parts of a person's life. The anticipation and memories that you have are some of the best. As a publisher of the Greater Than a Tourist book series, as well as the popular 50 Things to Know book series, we strive to help you learn about new places, spark your imagination, and inspire you. Wherever you are and whatever you do I wish you safe, fun, and inspiring travel.

Lisa Rusczyk Ed. D.
CZYK Publishing

OUR STORY

Traveling is a passion of the "Greater than a Tourist" series creator. Lisa studied abroad in college, and for their honeymoon Lisa and her husband toured Europe. During her travels to Malta, an older man tried to give her some advice based on his own experience living on the island since he was a young boy. She was not sure if she should talk to the stranger but was interested in his advice. When traveling to some places she was wary to talk to locals because she was afraid that they weren't being genuine. Through her travels, Lisa learned how much locals had to share with tourists. Lisa created the "Greater Than a Tourist" book series to help connect people with locals. A topic that locals are very passionate about sharing.

WELCOME TO
> TOURIST

INTRODUCTION

"Twenty years from now you will be more disappointed by the things you didn't do than by the ones you did do. So throw off the bowlines. Catch the trade winds in your sails. Explore. Dream. Discover."

– Mark Twain (Earth Trekkers)

Chester is one of the most beautiful and quaint places. This little city is full of history and life. It can provide someone with a nice, relaxing getaway with great sightseeing opportunities or a fun weekend out in the various pubs and clubs. Chester has a little bit of everything and offers great balance for a memorable trip.

1. FIND A PLACE TO STAY

Chester offers many hotels for guests to stay in. In city centre, the Grosvenor Hotel is a stunning four-star accommodation and perfectly located in the midst of the hustle and bustle.

If you have a smaller budget, many pubs, such as the George and Dragon, offer cozy upstairs rooms for a smaller price but also located in prime spots. They have history and good reviews. The interior designs of the bedrooms show off the history of the pubs and the area.

Airbnb's are located throughout the city in city centre or further away in quieter areas. I would suggest somewhere closer to town for easier access to all the sights and attractions.

2. GO TO A PUB

Throughout Chester, there are more pubs than I can count (probably). Pubs are sprinkled throughout the city, so a nice pub crawl is a great way to spend a day and find your favorite pub.

The Pied Bull is situated within the walls of the city and dates back to 1155. The interior design is reflective of its history with an original handmade staircase from 1533. It is a great place to book a room for a stay in Chester with a great brewery and beer terrace.

The Coach House Inn was voted Cheshire's Best Pub in 2016 and Best Accommodation in 2017. The inn has been in Chester since 1840 and is a great blend of traditional and modern. They offer a wonderful selection of real ales, selected wines, teas and coffees in the pub.

George and Dragon is considered the most haunted pub in Chester. It is said to be haunted by Roman Legionnaires because the pub is located on an old Roman road that the Legionnaires took from the north gate of the ancient Roman Chester fortress. The inside is cozy, and I spent the most time in this pub out of all the others. It is close to where I lived, has good food and drink for great prices, and friendly service. My roommate and I loved to share a bucket of chicken fingers and a side of chips. Their chips are amazing! The George also hosts quiz nights on Sundays which were always a blast to go to if we could get a team together. They also host a karaoke night and have two pool tables if anyone wants to play a game.

These are only a sampling of the available pubs in the city, each with their own history and atmosphere.

The pubs are all beautiful to look at due to their historical architecture and provide a warming and hearty interior.

3. HAVE A DONUT.

Dinky Donuts is an adorable hole in the wall by the clock tower in Chester. They make freshly baked donuts and are some of the most incredible donuts I have ever had. You get to choose between sugar coatings and Nutella add-ons. Dinky Donuts does a great 8 for £2.50 and 12 for £3.00 deal. They also sell ice cream!

4. TAKE A DIP

Many parts of Chester are surrounded by a scenic canal. There are precious little boats and sometimes ducks floating in the water. While it is not recommended to actually take a dip in the canal, it is a beautiful place to find a bench sit and eat lunch or enjoy the day. Many restaurants are located on the canal and give the best views for a romantic dinner.

The canal was built with the intention to connect Chester Middlewich but was not able to be completed due to some negotiation conflicts. Now the canal links Chester's River Dee to the south Cheshire town of Nantwich. It is not protected by the Chester Canal Heritage Trust which was set up in 1997 to promote the canal and its history.

5. WALK THE WALLS

The Walls of Chester are hundreds of years old and provide the perfect walking path. They take you above and around the city and end by the River Dee. I love walking the walls, and it was one of my favorite activities when the weather was nice. The Wall gives you access to different shops and cafes that you cannot see from street level. They also provide a stunning view of the city.

Their construction began in 70 A.D. and was completed in 80 A.D. by the Romans when they established the fortress of Deva. They are almost two miles in circumference and still have many of their medieval structures standing, such as Bonewaldesthorne's Tower, the Water Tower, Pemberton's Parlor, and Phoenix Tower.

6. GO TO CHURCH

Even for those who are not religious, the Chester Cathedral is a spectacle to be seen. Located in the city centre, its spires rise above the surrounding shops. The architecture of the façade is awe-inspiring and cannot go unnoticed. Inside the walls, pathways take you twisting and turning through the corridors. They allow tourists into the massive room where masses are held, and there is even a peaceful garden located in a center courtyard. They even have the Refectory Café and gift shop to visit after your tour. The cathedral never stopped taking my breath away, even though I passed it every day.

It was founded as a Benedictine abbey in 1092 in a Romanesque or Norman style, but was rebuilt with a more Gothic style beginning in 1250. This process took around 275 years and created the incredible cathedral that still stands today. The cathedral is the best venue in the city for orchestral performances, concerts, and fundraisers for charity. You can go to experience weekly organ recitals and choir shows.

7. VISIT A GARDEN

The Roman Gardens are located off the Walls past the clock and towards the river on the south east side of the city. They are lined with trees and hold ruins from Roman times. These columns and a small stage create a timeless little patch of grass that takes you back in time.

The gardens were constructed by Graham Webster in 1949 to display remaining fragments of ruins of the Roman fortress of Deva like the important military buildings, the main baths, and the legionary artifacts. These fragments were uncovered during a nineteenth century excavation in Chester. The gardens even include a reconstructed hypocaust with mosaics which was a Roman heating system that circulated hot air beneath the floor of a building to heat the room. This hypocaust

8. BE A ROMAN

Chester provides Roman tours to explore the Roman history that this city is rich with called the Dewa Roman Experience. Tour guides dress in Roman garb and take you through the entire city, pointing out important places with their swords and spilling all the fun facts about Roman Chester.

The Experience is located in the heart of the original legionary fortress and gives people the opportunity to see reconstructed Roman granaries, barracks, a bath house, tavern, market stalls, and even has an excavation site that allows viewings of genuine Roman, Saxon, and Medieval remains that are under Chester.

The hands-on room has won awards for allowing visitors to try on Roman armor, firing a catapult, building a hypocaust, and creating a mosaic. They even let you handle ancient pottery if you want some archaeology experience.

9. SEE A SHOW IN THE AMPHITHEATRE

Along with Roman tours, there is still an ancient Roman ampitheatre located in Chester. The historical society puts on shows there at scheduled times. There is a nice lawn to put out a blanket and enjoy the show. I was always entertained by these performances and even enjoyed just lounging in the grass and exploring the amphitheatre on my own when there was not a show going on.

The amphitheatre dates back to 86 A.D. and is the largest one excavated in all of the British Isles. It was built to entertain the 20th Legion who was stationed at the fort of Deva, but not all of the amphitheatre has been unearthed – the southern side of it is still hidden underground and creates the grassy hill for viewers to sit on.

10. VISIT THE MUSEUM

Founded in 1885, the Grosvenor Museum gives you another closer look into the history of Chester. It is a well laid out museum full of interesting artifacts and bits and baubles. They have a collection of Roman tombstones and exhibit the geology and natural history of Chester.

20 Castle Street lets you have a look into what a townhouse would look like from the 17th century to the 1920s and includes showing rooms that reveal what a Victorian kitchen, Georgian drawing room, nursery, and a completely furnished Edwardian bathroom.

The museum has over 100,000 visitors every year and has free admission. They even hold special events, activities, and workshops throughout the year. I think it is definitely a place worth going if you have a knack for history.

11. SEE A MOVIE OR BALLET

Chester has officially opened their multimillion theatre and library, The Storyhouse. This modern building has more activities than you would think could be put into one place. They show the newest movies, as well as putting on plays and ballets, serving as a well-stocked library, and even include a café and bar. The sprawling layout makes sure you never feel crammed, and I enjoyed going to see movies there and checking out books for my classes.

12. SEE A RACE

In the spring, Chester Racecourse opens and people flock in their best clothes to watch these races. It is the perfect excuse to be fancy, buy a big hat, and spend a day out on the town. The races are exciting and a big event in Chester.

The racecourse was established in 1539 and is the oldest racecourse still in use in Great Britain. Chester's racecourse has experienced some major events in the history of horse racing. It was at this racecourse that the first ever recorded prize was given to the winner of a horse race at the Chester Fair in 1512. By 1857, the races were big enough to make it economically viable for the first grandstand which allowed audiences to watch and enjoy all aspects of the races without feeling cramped. Currently, the biggest event happens in the beginning of May with a three-day festival that hosts historic races like the Chester Cup, the Chester Vase, the Ormande Stakes, the Cheshire Oaks, and the Dee Stakes.

13. CHECK OUT THE UNI CAMPUS

The University of Chester is located right outside of the city centre and within easy walking distance. There, you can find a number of soccer (or football as they would say) fields and a very nice campus. The Binks Building even has a Starbucks if you want to stop in on your walk. The campus has a nice balance of modern buildings and older, traditional stone ones. It is a beautiful campus.

14. HAVE A NIGHT OUT

Rosie's is one of the most prominent nightclubs in Chester. Three floors, each with their own genre of music, allow you to choose what you're in the mood to dance to. The first floor has some great throwback music, the second blasts the chart toppers, and the third is more for techno and drum and bass fans. It makes for a great night out, and I always loved going to Rosie's.

15. TRY QUID'S IN

Another big nightclub in Chester is Cruise. On Mondays, they have Quid's In where entrance is only £2. This club also three floors with the same music layout as Rosie's. Cruise's design is more modern and provides a more city feel than Rosie's. they have six different themed areas throughout the club, and you can reserve a booth for you and your friends in any of the themed rooms of your choice.

16. RECOVER FROM A NIGHT OUT WITH SOME PIZZA

Chester is home to Urbano 32, my favorite pizza place in the entire world. It is in a very central location and a very cool place to grab a bite. Their pizza menu is unique and delicious. The interior is rustic and industrial, and pizzas are made in the handmade clay pizza oven. They use local produce and have a delightful bar scene.

My favorite thing to order is the ricotta, spinach, black olives, garlic, tomato, and mozzarella pizza. My roommate and I always split a pizza with my half being that and hers being a margherita pizza with pepperoni. I get it every time, but you don't have to limit yourself to one thing. They have a wide variety of pizzas, antipastas, salads, and more. I have never been disappointed by a meal from Urbano.

17. WASH IT DOWN WITH A MILKSHAKE

Urbano 32's sister eatery is called Burger Shed and located very conveniently across the street. You can order a wide variety of different burgers that taste just as great as they sound on the menu. To finish off the meal, Burger Shed sells amazing milkshakes with all kinds of flavors – they even have a special section for shakes with an alcohol kick.

18. HAVE ANOTHER SHAKE

The Funky Cow is located near the Cathedral in a little back street, but they have the most amazing array of milkshake flavors and toppings. You can add as much to your milkshake as you want. They even offer a Vegemite shake, which I have never had the guts to order. I loved every shake I did get though! I seemed to favorite a

19. FINE DINE A WAFFLE

Off the Waffle is a scrumptious waffle shop where you can get waffles with crazy toppings. It's located – you guessed it – right off the wall. That means that on your way there, you can enjoy a nice stroll on the wall before diving into your waffle. Their menu expands to encompass crepes, coffees, teas, hot chocolates, milkshakes, and even savory waffles.

Some of their more extravagant waffles include the Oreo Crunch waffle topped with crushed Oreos, white

Belgian chocolate chips, and drizzled with chocolate sauce and the White Nutella waffles smothered in white Nutella spread, strawberry or banana slices, a topping of your choice, and completed with chocolate sauce.

20. ENJOY A CREPE INSTEAD

Crepeaffaire is a wonderful crepe restaurant that makes some of the yummiest crepes I have ever had. As an avid crepe lover, I visited Crepeaffaire more than I probably should have. They have everything from savory to sweet, so you can go in and a grab a bite no matter what kind of flavor you want.

21. CHOW DOWN ON A YORKSHIRE PUDDING

The York Roast Co. sells some of fillings Yorkshire puddings. Just the smell from the shop will draw you in. You can order a Yorkshire pudding wrap, which I had never seen anywhere else. The puddings are divine and a great way to fill your belly if you're looking for a hearty, warm meal. The menu is full of different options for these puddings, whether they are in wrap form or more traditional. The portions are massive and sure to fill you up.

22. GO DOWN TO THE RIVER

The River Dee is one of my favorite places in the entire world. Hands down, I love it so much. There is a precious gazebo that looks over the water and benches where you can enjoy the view. They have ice cream vendors and a little burger place on the road. The atmosphere at the River Dee is incomparable to anywhere else I have ever been. Everything about it is picturesque.

23. EAT AT HICKORY'S

Located right by the River, Hickory's has a gorgeous view of the water and serves the nicest ribs and other meaty treats. Their pulled pork sandwiches melt in your mouth and have the best sauce. They are an American style smokehouse with a vibrant menu that's worth ordering from. They serve big breakfasts, depending on what you choose to go with vegan and vegetarian options available. Their chicken fried waffle is served all day, so you if you're craving it after breakfast, you won't have to go without it.

Their main menu is based on larger meat dishes. They serve all kinds of briskets, baby back ribs, sausages, fajitas, steaks, burgers, and almost any other meatlover's desire. Their dessert menu is also pretty desirable and has so many different options to choose from. I am always a fan of their ice cream sandwich cookie.

They even offer some more Americanized drinks like different iced teas and lemonades in all kinds of flavors. You can choose from Blueberry Lemonade, Raspberry and Mint Lemonade, Pink Grapefruit Iced Tea, Peach and Passionfruit Iced Tea, and so many more! Personally, I love the Raspberry and Mint Lemonade. It is one of the most refreshing drinks I have ever had. Of course, they have other drinks too like cocktails, ales, beers, milkshakes, and other nonalcoholic beverages.

Hickory's has an amazing location right on the River Dee, so on a nice day, you can sit outside and watch the activity going past on the water or on the sidewalks. It was so relaxing and always a great time.

24. RENT A PADDLEBOAT

On warm, sunny days, renting a paddleboat or rowboat on the River is a must. I rented a rowboat for an hour with some friends, and we had the best time trying to navigate our way on the river. We were treated with great views of the riverbanks and lots of laughter. I recommend this activity whole-heartedly.

The paddleboat might be the easier option, but it costs a few more pounds to rent one of them. It's best to get there early or wait for a less busy time in order to avoid waiting in longer lines. The experience is worth the wait though, so don't pass it up! You'll make memories you'll never forget.

25. TAKE A BOAT TOUR

On the river, they offer great ferry tours on boats like the Mark Twain and the Jackie. These ferries will take you down the river and give you amazing views of the houses on the banks and the Meadows. The best part is you don't have to walk! Personally, I love walking, but I think the tours are super fun and another way to spend a spring day in Chester.

You can easily find the prices and which tour you would like to take online. Since it's England, and there is always a chance of rain, these boats have a nice interior that would shade you from the rain if the clouds decide to open on your tour.

26. CROSS THE BRIDGE

The Chester Bridge spans over the River Dee and takes you to its other shores where there is less going on, but still an enjoyable time. There is a nice trail that takes you down the river that is spotted with benches for easy relaxation with a view. It is a great place to sit and eat your ice cream cone, which I have done on many occasions.

27. TAKE A SCENIC NATURE WALK

Across the bridge, I love to turn left and wander as far as possible. This trail takes you to the Meadows, which is one of the reasons that I find the River Dee so charming. In spring, flowers are blooming, and the grass is green. The walk is calming and beautiful. The path is flat and easy to walk with no hills, but it can get a little muddy if there was a heavy rain. This issue can be avoided as long as you pick a nice day to take a walk. There are all kinds of things trees, flowers, and things going on in the River to look at. Often, the rowing team was having practice, so you can try to race them (if you're feeling up to it). If you want to have a long walk, make sure you pack your own water. The Meadows don't have any place to stop and buy a drink. They leave the attractions and places like that on the other side of the bridge.

I loved taking little picnics and finding the perfect spot on the river to spread out a blanket and have some lunch with my friends. The houses on the river are amazing. Their architecture is so unique, and many have their backyards terraced which is stunning to look at. My friend and I loved walking through the Meadows and pointing out which houses we loved.

28. SIP ON A MOJITO

Off the Wall is a bar that is unsurprisingly located right off the wall. They have interesting drinks to say the least, such as a jelly bean pitcher which is one of the sweetest drinks I have ever had. Only try it if you have a big sweet tooth. My favorite drink is their passionfruit mojito. I highly recommend. The drinks can be on the pricier side, but the food is cheap and tasty. It is also a decent place for a night out. They play good music and keep the drinks going. You can even try some of their more experimental shots like the bubblegum shot! They have a whole list, so you and your friends can each try a new, fun flavor.

29. COMBINE CHEMISTRY AND DRINKING

One of the more expensive places you can get a drink in Chester is the Alchemist. This nifty bar uses all kinds of unique methods to create their drinks. They serve a color changing drink, a flavor changing one (raspberry to chocolate), and one that has small gold flakes swirling around in it. The bar is chic and offers a more sophisticated vibe. Their drink menu leaves you wondering which magical drink to try next. And if you're a bit peckish, they have a smaller menu of appetizers to munch on while you have your drinks. The mac and cheese bites are delicious.

30. TRY OUT FLOWERS AND TEA

The Flower Cup is one of the cutest places I have ever been. This aesthetically pleasing tea shop sells an assortment of teas and foods while selling little plants at the front of the shop. I bought two succulents there – both still alive. You can also buy cactuses and some larger plants.

Their menu is mostly made up of sandwiches and other lighter foods. This is not a sit-down for a meal place but rather a place to spend a quiet afternoon with a pot of a tea and some good chatter with a friend. The food that they do have is light and crisp and tastes amazing. I thoroughly enjoy the sandwiches I get every time I go.

The Flower Cup is a wonderful spot to stop for a cup of tea, and the service is always friendly. It is a great place to take a few pictures for your Instagram or travel blog.

31. TRY MORE FLOWERS AND FOOD

The Botanist is a bit more than a tea shop. This restaurant does not sell flowers, but their décor inside is very enticing. The Botanist has a very pleasing atmosphere with its low lighting and serves great food. This is an amazing place to get dinner with great service. When you sit down, there is something pretty to look at no matter where you look. The decorations have an earthy, outdoorsy vibe, but they remain elegant at the same time. Their menu has a variety of dishes, each one tasty. I have been there on multiple occasions and enjoyed it every time. More of a sit down and dine kind of place, I really enjoyed the paella that I ordered there.

32. EAT AT A TAVERN

The City Tavern was my favorite place to eat while I lived in Chester. The food is reasonably priced and tastes great. The inside is warm and welcoming with second floor seating for more seclusion. The beer garden outside shows all the football games and is surrounded by twinkly lights. Their strawberry daiquiris are amazing, and I always made sure to grab them with their 2 for 1 special. I'm a sucker for mac and cheese, and it quickly became my go-to order there. They also have great burgers and halloumi. If you've never tried halloumi, I highly recommend it. I'd never heard of it until living in England, but it is a unique experience. I can honestly say that I have never tried another food quite like it, but the best halloumi I've ever had was at the City Tavern. I have a lot of great memories at this tavern, and I think it is a very special place.

33. GO INDOOR SHOPPING

The Grosvenor Shopping Centre has a bunch of different stores from Sports Direct to Topshop to Build-A-Bear to T.K. Maxx (better known is T.J. Maxx in the United States. If you are in need of something, you can probably find it in the shopping centre. There is also a Costa for a quick drink and a little bakery that sells enormous cookie cakes.

34. GO OUTDOOR SHOPPING

The city centre is sprawling with all kinds of shops. Chester has Primark, River Island, New Look,

Debenhams's, Rolex, Lush, more obscure boutiques, charity and vintage shops, and countless others. There is even a Liverpool football store for all your football team needs. I loved popping from shop to shop and checking out the different stores. There are street level shops and second level shops that you can't miss out on. Cafes are dotted in between shops and are perfect for a rest while shopping or a quick bite.

In general, Chester is a beautifully historic city, so even without shopping, it was interesting to go from shop to shop and see how their interior was created to fit with the historic shapes of the buildings. Each shop has its own unique look, and some may look modern on the outside and have a rich, older look inside, or vice versa. Every shop in Chester has character, and I loved wandering the streets whenever I could. I always discovered a new place to check out.

35. VISIT THE MARKET

The Chester Market is a great way to do some market shopping. You can get your groceries there from cheese shops and fruit and veggie stands. This gives a fun shopping experience instead of going to Tesco or some other chain grocery store. This gives a more authentic feel to your shopping, and they and sell different wares for all of the different holidays. I recommend checking Chester out during the winter holiday season, not only for the fun deals in the Market, but all over Chester, there is a festive atmosphere and decorations.

36. DO SOME MORE SHOPPING

Any shop that you don't find in Chester, you'll find in Cheshire Oaks. This shopping outlet is located a little out of the city but is an easy bus ride away and has over 130 different outlet shops. You'll find even more shopping in a more suburban than city setting. The outlet has Converse, Levi's, Nike Factory, Pandora, Polo Ralph Lauren, Calvin Klein, Michael Kohrs, and more. It is located near some more chain food places like Pizza Hut, TGI Fridays, and more. Cheshire Oaks is a good day out if you want to do some window or actual shopping.

37. GO SEE A MOVIE

Also located in Cheshire Oaks is the Vue cinema. This movie theater will show all the new movies, while the Storyhouse only shows a select few and gears more towards indie movies. This is your regular movie theater and a good way to spend a rainy afternoon if you want to see a film that has just been released. They do a special on Mondays, so you can get cheaper tickets!

38. SEE SOME BIRDS

Located at the back of the Cathedral and right off the wall is a falconry. This gives you an up close and personal look at these incredible birds. They give shows and talks and showcase some more animals and plants. Visiting the falconry is a fun and educational way to spend a few hours on a beautiful day where you don't want to be stuck indoors.

39. VISIT THE ZOO

To see an even greater array of wildlife, feel free to visit the Chester Zoo. It is counted as one of the best zoos in the United Kingdom and the largest. It covers over 100 acres and total land holding of 400 acres. It was founded in the early 1930s and is now run by the North of England Zoological Society. This zoo will take you an entire day to get through and is full of vibrant animal life with over 500 species and over 80 acres of stunning garden space. The Chester Zoo is very active in global wildlife conservation programs.

There is a bat cave experience where you and your friends/family walk in the dark while bats fly all around you. It's harmless, but still gets your heart racing. On a calmer note, they also have a butterfly room where you can enjoy a light stroll through some flowers and wait for a butterfly to land on you if you stay still enough. Chester has one of the largest collections of birds and an overhead Monorail to take you through the zoo.

I spent a day at the zoo with my friends, and we had so much fun. To save some money, we packed our own lunches, as the zoo's food tends to be a bit pricier. This was great because we also packed snacks to munch on during the walk. We got great pictures with the animals and some pretty up close and personal experiences. One of my friends even kissed a penguin – through the glass of course! I have a cool picture of my hand up against a chimp's on the glass. He was very interested in our group and wasn't afraid to "talk" with us.

40. GO TO THE AQUARIUM

The Blue Planet Aquarium is another place to see some creatures, though this time they are aquatic. It is also the largest aquarium in the United Kingdom and has two floors of interactive displays and exhibits. The aquarium is located a bit outside of the city in Ellesmere Port but is still easily reached by bus or short car journey.

There are more sharks in this aquarium than anywhere else in England with more than ten species from different places around the world. Their Aquatunnel is a moving walkway over seventy meters long that gives an amazing underwater experience. There's even a Caribbean themed restaurant and gift shop for when you get in the mood for food.

41. TRY FARM ANIMALS AND ICE CREAM

The Chester Ice Cream Farm is a further outside of Chester, but reachable through public transit. This farm includes unique flavors of ice creams, as well as having a petting zoo. Entrance is free and fun for the whole family.

42. SEE SOME BIGGER GARDENS

The Ness Botanic Gardens of property of the University of Liverpool and are some of the most beautiful botanic gardens covering 64 acres. Founded in 1898, the gardens have an array of shrubs, trees, rhododendrons, azaleas, and a tranquil water garden. The Four Seasons Café is a great addition to this already stunning location. Their vegetation is breathtaking, and as a plant lover, I loved visiting. I think that this excursion is worth it for the beauty.

43. GO TO WALES

The Wales Coast Path begins in Chester and takes you all the way to the coast of Wales. You have to be in shape for this kind of walking, but it is definitely worth it for the views. Fans of outdoor adventure should be all over this walking trail as a challenging venture while in Chester.

44. VISIT A CASTLE

Beeston Castle is a short trip outside of Chester and gives you a look at how grand life used to be. This historic castle provides tours of the grounds and many picture opportunities. The castle looms 350 feet above the surrounding landscape and demands attention.

Built in 1225, this structure was used as a fortress in the Bronze Age and became an important metal-working site then a hillfort in the Iron Age. The castle was founded by Ranulf, the sixth Earl of Chester who granted the land it is built on after returning from the Fifth Crusade. In the medieval documents, it is referred to as the Castle on the Rock – "Castellum de Rupe."

A museum located in a modern extension of the nineteenth century gatehouse retells the 4,000-year-old story of this castle through display models and other artifacts.

Outside of the city, seeing this structure standing on its own is a jaw-dropping sight.

45. WALK THROUGH THE FOREST

The Delamere Forest is another nature lovers dream. This area is towered over by ancient trees and allows for relaxing walks on paths through the foliage and owned by the Forestry Commission. There are even paths for cyclers. The forest covers 2,400 acres of land and is Cheshire's largest remaining woodland. Within the forest there are two lakes – Blakemere Moss and Black Lake. Both are designated as Sites of Special Scientific Interest. It is just another great way to spend a day outdoors.

46. BE A HARRY STYLES FAN

Chester is a short fifteen-minute train ride away from Harry Styles' hometown of Holmes Chapel,

Cheshire. You can visit the bakery where he worked and then spend a quiet hour or two at a café or tea shop in the small town. This is not a trip for everyone, but a very exciting detail for a few.

47. VISIT LIVERPOOL

If you want to avoid staying in a big city, but still want to visit, Chester is the perfect place. It is close to Liverpool, which is a beautiful city with fun activities to do. I visited Liverpool a few times while in Chester and enjoyed it every time, but by far preferred the charisma and charm of Chester. Liverpool served as a great outing for a day.

48. VISIT MANCHESTER

Manchester follows the same principles as Liverpool, but I found that there was much less to do in Manchester. It was a fun day trip, but again, actually being immersed in Chester was better. There is a definite busy city feeling in Manchester that can be exciting.

49. DON'T BE AFRAID TO TRY NEW THINGS

Chester is filled to the brim with unique experiences. Visit everywhere that you can. I lived there for five months and still feel like I missed out on a few things. I cannot wait to go back. The city itself is so charming and full of life, but not in a way that ever makes you feel overwhelmed.

50. HAVE FUN AND EAT A LOT

In Chester, there are so many places to eat. I was constantly eating in new places while I was there. Try to avoid chain food places like Nando's and McDonald's. Branch out and try the local restaurants and little shops. There is so much to experience in this little city.

TOP REASONS TO BOOK THIS TRIP

Food: Incredible pubs, taverns, bars, and restaurants.

Atmosphere: No other city in the world feels the same as Chester.

History: Chester is full of rich history that can be seen in its architecture and streets.

OTHER RESOURCES:

https://www.visitcheshire.com/chester

https://www.historic-uk.com/HistoryMagazine/DestinationsUK/Chester/

https://www.visitbritain.com/gb/en/england/northern-england/chester

BONUS BOOK

50 THINGS TO KNOW ABOUT PACKING LIGHT FOR TRAVEL

PACK THE RIGHT WAY EVERY TIME

AUTHOR: MANIDIPA BHATTACHARYYA

Edited by Melanie Howthorne

ABOUT THE AUTHOR

Manidipa Bhattacharyya is a creative writer and editor, with an education in English literature and Linguistics. After working in the IT industry for seven long years she decided to call it quits and follow her heart instead. Manidipa has been ghost writing, editing, proof reading and doing secondary research services for many story tellers and article writers for about three years. She stays in Kolkata, India with her husband and a busy two year old. In her own time Manidipa enjoys travelling, photography and writing flash fiction.

Manidipa believes in travelling light and never carries anything that she couldn't haul herself on a trip. However, travelling with her child changed the scenario. She seemed to carry the entire world with her for the baby on the first two trips. But good sense prevailed and she is again working her way to becoming a light traveler, this time with a kid.

INTRODUCTION

He who would travel happily
must travel light.

-Antoine de Saint-Exupéry

Travel takes you to different places from seas and mountains to deserts and much more. In your travels you get to interact with different people and their cultures. You will, however, enjoy the sights and interact positively with these new people even more, if you are travelling light.

When you travel light your mind can be free from worry about your belongings. You do not have to spend precious vacation time waiting for your luggage to arrive after a long flight. There is be no chance of your bags going missing and the best part is that you need not pay a fee for checked baggage.

People who have mastered this art of packing light will root for you to take only one carry-on, wherever you go. However, many people can find it really hard to pack light. More so if you are travelling with children. Differentiating between “must have” and “just in case” items is the starting point. There will be ample shopping avenues at your destination which are just waiting to be explored.

This book will show you ‘packing’ in a new ‘light’ – pun intended – and help you to embrace light packing practices for all of your future travels.

Off to packing!

DEDICATION

I dedicate this book to all the travel buffs that I know, who have given me great insights into the contents of their backpacks.

THE RIGHT TRAVEL GEAR

1. CHOOSE YOUR TRAVEL GEAR CAREFULLY

While selecting your travel gear, pick items that are light weight, durable and most importantly, easy to carry. There are cases with wheels so you can drag them along – these are usually on the heavy side because of the trolley. Alternatively a backpack that you can carry comfortably on your back, or even a duffel bag that you can carry easily by hand or sling across your body are also great options. Whatever you choose, one thing to keep in mind is that the luggage itself should not weigh a ton, this will give you the flexibility to bring along one extra pair of shoes if you so desire.

2. CARRY THE MINIMUM NUMBER OF BAGS

Selecting light weight luggage is not everything. You need to restrict the number of bags you carry as well. One carry-on size bag is ideal for light travel. Most carriers allow one cabin baggage plus one purse, handbag or camera bag as long as it slides under the seat in front. So technically, you can carry two items of luggage without checking them in.

3. PACK ONE EXTRA BAG

Always pack one extra empty bag along with your essential items. This could be a very light weight duffel bag or even a sturdy tote bag which takes up minimal space. In the event that you end up buying a lot of souvenirs, you already have a handy bag to stuff all that into and do not have to spend time hunting for an appropriate bag.

I'm very strict with my packing and have everything in its right place. I never change a rule. I hardly use anything in the hotel room. I wheel my own wardrobe in and that's it.

Charlie Watts

CLOTHES & ACCESSORIES

4. PLAN AHEAD

Figure out in advance what you plan to do on your trip. That will help you to pick that one dress you need for the occasion. If you are going to attend a wedding then you have to carry formal wear. If not, you can ditch the gown for something lighter that will be comfortable during long walks or on the beach.

5. WEAR THAT JACKET

Remember that wearing items will not add extra luggage for your air travel. So wear that bulky jacket that you plan to carry for your trip. This saves space and can also help keep you warm during the chilly flight.

6. MIX AND MATCH

Carry clothes that can be interchangeably used to reinvent your look. Find one top that goes well with a couple of pairs of pants or skirts. Use tops, shirts and jackets wisely along with other accessories like a scarf or a stole to create a new look.

7. CHOOSE YOUR FABRIC WISELY

Stuffing clothes in cramped bags definitely takes its toll which results in wrinkles. It is best to carry wrinkle free, synthetic clothes or merino tops. This will eliminate the need for that small iron you usually bring along.

8. DITCH CLOTHES PACK UNDERWEAR

Pack more underwear and socks. These are the things that will give you a fresh feel even if you do not get a chance to wear fresh clothes. Moreover these are easy to wash and can be dried inside the hotel room itself.

9. CHOOSE DARK OVER LIGHT

While picking your clothes choose dark coloured ones. They are easy to colour coordinate and can last longer before needing a wash. Accidental food spills and dirt from the road are less visible on darker clothes.

10. WEAR YOUR JEANS

Take only one pair of Jeans with you, which you should wear on the flight. Remember to pick a pair that can be worn for sightseeing trips and is equally eloquent for dinner. You can add variety by adding light weight cargoes and chinos.

11. CARRY SMART ACCESSORIES

The right accessory can give you a fresh look even with the same old dress. An intelligent neck-piece, a couple of bright scarves, stoles or a sarong can be used in a number of ways to add variety to your clothing. These light weight beauties can double up as a nursing cover, a light blanket, beach wear, a modesty cover for visiting places of worship, and also makes for an enthralling game of peek-a-boo.

12. LEARN TO FOLD YOUR GARMENTS

Seasoned travellers all swear by rolling their clothes for compact and wrinkle free packing. Bundle packing, where you roll the clothes around a central object as if tying it up, is also a popular method of compact and wrinkle free packing. Stacking folded clothes one on top of another is a big no-no as it makes creases extreme and they are difficult to get rid of without ironing.

13. WASH YOUR DIRTY LAUNDRY

One of the ways to avoid carrying loads of clothes is to wash the clothes you carry. At some places you might get to use the laundry services or a Laundromat but if you are in a pinch, best solution is to wash them yourself. If that is the plan then carrying quick drying clothes is highly recommended, which most often also happen to be the wrinkle free variety.

14. LEAVE THOSE TOWELS BEHIND

Regular towels take up a lot of space, are heavy and take ages to dry out. If you are staying at hotels they will provide you with towels anyway. If you are travelling to a remote place, where the availability of towels look doubtful, carry a light weight travel towel of viscose material to do the job.

15. USE A COMPRESSION BAG

Compression bags are getting lots of recommendation now days from regular travellers. These are useful for saving space in your luggage when you have to pack bulky dresses. While packing for the return trip, get help from the hotel staff to arrange a vacuum cleaner.

FOOTWEAR

16. PUT ON YOUR HIKING BOOTS

If you have plans to go hiking or trekking during your trip, you will need those bulky hiking boots. The best way to carry them is to wear them on flight to save space and luggage weight. You can remove the boots once inside and be comfortable in your socks.

17. PICKING THE RIGHT SHOES

Shoes are often the bulkiest items, along with being the dainty if you are a female. They need care and take up a lot of space in your luggage. It is advisable therefore to pick shoes very carefully. If you plan to do a lot of walking and site seeing, then wearing a pair of comfortable walking shoes are a must. For more formal occasions you can carry durable, light weight flats which will not take up much space.

18. STUFF SHOES

If you happen to pack a pair of shoes, ensure you utilize their hollow insides. Tuck small items like rolled up socks or belts to save space. They will also be easy to find.

TOILETRIES

19. STASHING TOILETRIES

Carry only absolute necessities. Airline rules dictate that for one carry-on bag, liquids and gels must be in 3.4 ounce (100ml) bottles or less, and must be packed in a one quart zip-lock bag. If you are planning to stay in a hotel, the basic things will be provided for you. It's best is to buy the rest from the local market at your destination.

20. TAKE ALONG TAMPONS

Tampons are a hard to find item in a lot of countries. Figure out how many you need and pack accordingly. For longer stays you can buy them online and have them delivered to where you are staying.

21. GET PAMPERED BEFORE YOU TRAVEL

Some avid travellers suggest getting a pedicure and manicure just the day before travelling. This not only gives you a well kept look, you also save the trouble of packing nail polish. Remember, every little bit of weight reduced adds up.

ELECTRONICS

22. LUGGING ALONG ELECTRONICS

Electronics have a large role to play in our lives today. Most of us cannot imagine our lives away from our phones, laptops or tablets. However while travelling, one must consider the amount of weight these electronics add to our luggage. Thankfully smart phones come along with all the essentials tools like a camera, email access, picture editing tools and more. They are smart to the point of eliminating the need to carry multiple gadgets. Choose a smart phone that suits all your requirements and travel with the world in your palms or pocket.

23. REDUCE THE NUMBER OF CHARGERS

If you do travel with multiple electronic devices, you will have to bear the additional burden of carrying all their chargers too. Check if a single charger can be used for multiple devices. You might also consider investing in a pocket charger. These small devices support multiple devices while keeping you charged on the go.

24. TRAVEL FRIENDLY APPS

Along with smart phones come numerous apps, which are immensely helpful in our travels. You name it and you have an app for it at hand – take pictures, sharing with friends and family, torch to light dark roads, maps, checking flight/train times, find hotels and many other things. Use these smart alternatives to traditional items like books to eliminate weight and save space.

I get ideas about what's essential when packing my suitcase.

-Diane von Furstenberg

TRAVELLING WITH KIDS

25. BRING ALONG THE STROLLER

Kids might enjoy walking for a while but they soon tire out and a stroller is the just the right thing for them to rest in while you continue your tour. Strollers also double duty as a luggage carrier and shopping bag holder. Remember to pick a light weight, easy to handle brand of stroller. Better yet, find out in advance if you can rent a stroller at your destination.

26. BRING ONLY ENOUGH DIAPERS FOR YOUR TRIP

Diapers take up a lot of space and add to the weight of your luggage. Therefore it is advisable to carry just enough diapers to last through the trip and a few for afterwards, till you buy fresh stock at your destination. Unless of course you are travelling to a really remote area, in which case you have no choice but to carry the load. Otherwise diapers are something you will find pretty easily.

27. TAKE ONLY A COUPLE OF TOYS

Children are easily attracted by new things in their environment. While travelling they will find numerous 'new' objects to scrutinize and play with. Packing just one favorite toy is enough, or if there is no favorite toy leave out all of them in favor of stories or imaginary games.

28. CARRY KID FRIENDLY SNACKS

Create a small snack counter in your bag to store away quick bites for those sudden hunger pangs. Depending on the child's age this could include chocolates, raisins, dry fruits, granola bars or biscuits. Also keep a bottle of water handy for your little one.

These things do not add much weight and can be adjusted in a handbag or knapsack.

29. GAMES TO CARRY

Create some travel specific, imaginary games if you have slightly grown up children, like spot the attractions. Keep a coloring book and colors handy for in-flight or hotel time. Apps on your smart phone can keep the children engaged with cartoons and story books. Older children are often entertained by games available on phones or tablets. This cuts the weight of luggage down while keeping the kids entertained.

30. LET THE KIDS CARRY THEIR LOAD

A good thing is to start early sharing of responsibilities. Let your child pick a bag of his or her choice and pack it themselves. Keep tabs on what they are stuffing in their bags by asking if they will be using that item on the trip. It could start out being just an entertainment bag initially but with growing years they will learn to sort the useful from the superfluous. Children as little as four can maneuver a small trolley suitcase like a pro- their experience in pull along toys credit. If you are worried that you may be pulling it for them, you may want to start with a backpack.

31. DECIDE ON LOCATION FOR CHILDREN TO SLEEP

While on a trip you might not always get a crib at your destination, and carrying one will make life all the more difficult. Instead call ahead to see if there are any cribs or roll out beds for children. You may even put blankets on the floor. Weave them a story about camping and they will gladly sleep without any trouble.

32. GET BABY PRODUCTS DELIVERED AT YOUR DESTINATION

If you are absolutely paranoid about not getting your favourite variety of diaper or brand of baby food, check out online stores like amazon.com for services in your destination city. You can buy things online ahead of your travel and get them delivered to your hotel upon arrival.

33. FEEDING NEEDS OF YOUR INFANTS

If you are travelling with a breastfed infant, you save the trouble of carrying bottles and bottle sanitization kits. For special food, or medications, you may need to call ahead to make sure you have a refrigerator where you are staying.

34. FEEDING NEEDS OF YOUR TODDLER

With the progression from infancy to toddler, their dietary requirements too evolve. You will have to pack some snacks for travelling time. Fresh fruits and vegetables can be purchased at your destination. Most of the cities you travel to in whichever part of the world, will have baby food products and formulas, available at the local drug-store or the supermarket.

35. PICKING CLOTHES FOR YOUR BABY

Contrary to popular belief, babies can do without many changes of clothes. At the most pack 2 outfits per day. Pack mix and match type clothes for your little one as well. Pick things which are comfortable to wear and quick to dry.

36. SELECTING SHOES FOR YOUR BABY

Like outfits, kids can make do with two pairs of comfortable shoes. If you can get some water resistant shoes it will be best. To expedite drying wet shoes, you can stuff newspaper in them then wrap them with newspaper and leave them to dry overnight.

37. KEEP ONE CHANGE OF CLOTHES HANDY

Travelling with kids can be tricky. Keep a change of clothes for the kids and mum handy in your purse or tote bag. This takes a bit of space in your hand luggage but comes extremely handy in case there are any accidents or spills.

38. LEAVE BEHIND BABY ACCESSORIES

Baby accessories like their bed, bath tub, car seat, crib etc. should be left at home. Many hotels provide a crib on request, while car seats can be borrowed from friends or rented. Babies can be given a bath in the hotel sink or even in the adult bath tub with a little bit of water. If you bring a few bath toys, they can be used in the bath, pool, and out of water. They can also be sanitized easily in the sink.

39. CARRY A SMALL LOAD OF PLASTIC BAGS

With children around there are chances of a number of soiled clothes and diapers. These plastic bags help to sort the dirt from the clean inside your big bag.

These are very light weight and come in handy to other carry stuff as well at times.

PACK WITH A PURPOSE

40. PACKING FOR BUSINESS TRIPS

One neutral-colored suit should suffice. It can be paired with different shirts, ties and accessories for different occasions. One pair of black suit pants could be worn with a matching jacket for the office or with a snazzy top for dinner.

41. PACKING FOR A CRUISE

Most cruises have formal dinners, and that formal dress usually takes up a lot of space. However you might find a tuxedo to rent. For women, a short black dress with multiple accessory options will do the trick.

42. PACKING FOR A LONG TRIP OVER DIFFERENT CLIMATES

The secret packing mantra for travel over multiple climates is layering. Layering traps air around your body creating insulation against the cold. The same light t-shirt that is comfortable in a warmer climate can be the innermost layer in a colder climate.

REDUCE SOME MORE WEIGHT

43. LEAVE PRECIOUS THINGS AT HOME

Things that you would hate to lose or get damaged leave them at home. Precious jewelry, expensive gadgets or dresses, could be anything. You will not require these on your trip. Leave them at home and spare the load on your mind.

44. SEND SOUVENIRS BY MAIL

If you have spent all your money on purchasing souvenirs, carrying them back in the same bag that you brought along would be difficult. Either pack everything in another bag and check it in the airport or get everything shipped to your home. Use an international carrier for a secure transit, but this could be more expensive than the checking fees at the airport.

45. AVOID CARRYING BOOKS

Books equal to weight. There are many reading apps which you can download on your smart phone or tab.

Plus there are gadgets like Kindle and Nook that are thinner and lighter alternatives to your regular book.

CHECK, GET, SET, CHECK AGAIN

46. STRATEGIZE BEFORE PACKING

Create a travel list and prepare all that you think you need to carry along. Keep everything on your bed or floor before packing and then think through once again – do I really need that? Any item that meets this question can be avoided. Remove whatever you don't really need and pack the rest.

47. TEST YOUR LUGGAGE

Once you have fully packed for the trip take a test trip with your luggage. Take your bags and go to town for window shopping for an hour. If you enjoy your hour long trip it is good to go, if not, go home and reduce the load some more. Repeat this test till you hit the right weight.

48. ADD A ROLL OF DUCT TAPE

You might wonder why, when this book has been talking about reducing stuff, we're suddenly asking you to pack something totally unusual. This is because when you have limited supplies, duct tape is immensely helpful for small repairs – a broken bag, leaking zip-lock bag, broken sunglasses, you name it and duct tape can fix it, temporarily.

49. LIST OF ESSENTIAL ITEMS

Even though the emphasis is on packing light, there are things which have to be carried for any trip. Here is our list of essentials:

- Passport/Visa or any other ID
- Any other paper work that might be required on a trip like permits, hotel reservation confirmations etc.
- Medicines – all your prescription medicines and emergency kit, especially if you are travelling with children
- Medical or vaccination records
- Money in foreign currency if travelling to a different country
- Tickets- Email or Message them to your phone

50. MAKE THE MOST OF YOUR TRIP

Wherever you are going, whatever you hope to do we encourage you to embrace it whole-heartedly. Take in the scenery, the culture and above all, enjoy your time away from home.

On a long journey even a straw weighs heavy.

-Spanish Proverb

PACKING AND PLANNING TIPS

A Week before Leaving

- Arrange for someone to take care of pets and water plants.
- Stop mail and newspaper.
- Notify Credit Card companies where you are going.
- Change your thermostat settings.
- Car inspected, oil is changed, and tires have the correct pressure.
- Passports and photo identification is up to date.
- Pay bills.
- Copy important items and download travel Apps.
- Start collecting small bills for tips.

Right Before Leaving

- Clean out refrigerator.
- Empty garbage cans.
- Lock windows.
- Make sure you have the proper identification with you.
- Bring cash for tips.
- Remember travel documents.
- Lock door behind you.
- Remember wallet.
- Unplug items in house and pack chargers.

>TOURIST

READ OTHER GREATER THAN A TOURIST BOOKS

Greater Than a Tourist San Miguel de Allende Guanajuato Mexico: 50 Travel Tips from a Local by Tom Peterson

Greater Than a Tourist – Lake George Area New York USA: 50 Travel Tips from a Local by Janine Hirschklau

Greater Than a Tourist – Monterey California United States: 50 Travel Tips from a Local by Katie Begley

Greater Than a Tourist – Chanai Crete Greece: 50 Travel Tips from a Local by Dimitra Papagrigoraki

Greater Than a Tourist – The Garden Route Western Cape Province South Africa: 50 Travel Tips from a Local by Li-Anne McGregor van Aardt

Greater Than a Tourist – Sevilla Andalusia Spain: 50 Travel Tips from a Local by Gabi Gazon

Greater Than a Tourist – Kota Bharu Kelantan Malaysia: 50 Travel Tips from a Local by Aditi Shukla

Children's Book: Charlie the Cavalier Travels the World by Lisa Rusczyk

>TOURIST

> TOURIST

Visit Greater Than a Tourist for Free Travel Tips http://GreaterThanATourist.com

Sign up for the Greater Than a Tourist Newsletter for discount days, new books, and travel information: http://eepurl.com/cxspyf

Follow us on Facebook for tips, images, and ideas: https://www.facebook.com/GreaterThanATourist

Follow us on Pinterest for travel tips and ideas: http://pinterest.com/GreaterThanATourist

Follow us on Instagram for beautiful travel images: http://Instagram.com/GreaterThanATourist

>TOURIST

> TOURIST

Please leave your honest review of this book on Amazon and Goodreads. Please send your feedback to GreaterThanaTourist@gmail.com as we continue to improve the series. We appreciate your positive and constructive feedback. Thank you.

METRIC CONVERSIONS

TEMPERATURE

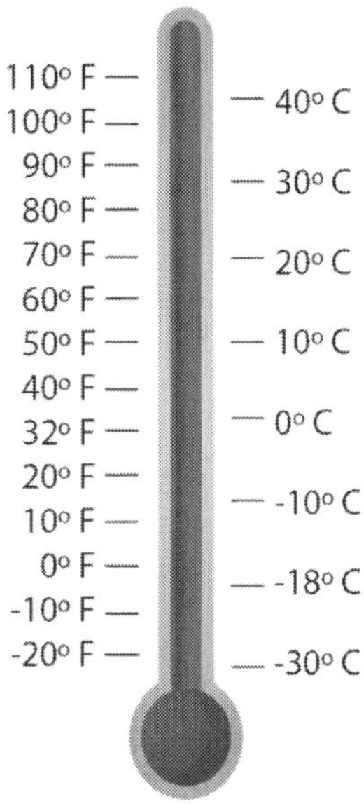

To convert F to C:

Subtract 32, and then multiply by 5/9 or .5555.

To Convert C to F:

Multiply by 1.8 and then add 32.

32F = 0C

LIQUID VOLUME

To Convert:....................Multiply by

U.S. Gallons to Liters................. 3.8

U.S. Liters to Gallons 26

Imperial Gallons to U.S. Gallons 1.2

Imperial Gallons to Liters....... 4.55

Liters to Imperial Gallons 22

1 Liter = .26 U.S. Gallon

1 U.S. Gallon = 3.8 Liters

DISTANCE

To convert ....Multiply by

Inches to Centimeters 2.54

Centimeters to Inches 39

Feet to Meters........................ .3

Meters to Feet 3.28

Yards to Meters 91

Meters to Yards 1.09

Miles to Kilometers 1.61

Kilometers to Miles............ .62

1 Mile = 1.6 km

1 km = .62 Miles

WEIGHT

1 Ounce = .28 Grams

1 Pound = .4555 Kilograms

1 Gram = .04 Ounce

1 Kilogram = 2.2 Pounds

TRAVEL QUESTIONS

- Do you bring presents home to family or friends after a vacation?
- Do you get motion sick?
- Do you have a favorite billboard?
- Do you know what to do if there is a flat tire?
- Do you like a sun roof open?
- Do you like to eat in the car?
- Do you like to wear sun glasses in the car?
- Do you like toppings on your ice cream?
- Do you use public bathrooms?
- Did you bring your cell phone and does it have power?
- Do you have a form of identification with you?
- Have you ever been pulled over by a cop?
- Have you ever given money to a stranger on a road trip?
- Have you ever taken a road trip with animals?
- Have you ever went on a vacation alone?
- Have you ever run out of gas?

- If you could move to any place in the world, where would it be?
- If you could travel anywhere in the world, where would you travel?
- If you could travel in any vehicle, which one would it be?
- If you had three things to wish for from a magic genie, what would they be?
- If you have a driver's license, how many times did it take you to pass the test?
- What are you the most afraid of on vacation?
- What do you want to get away from the most when you are on vacation?
- What foods smells bad to you?
- What item do you bring on ever trip with you away from home?
- What makes you sleepy?
- What song would you love to hear on the radio when you're cruising on the highway?
- What travel job would you want the least?
- What will you miss most while you are away from home?
- What is something you always wanted to try?

- What is the best road side attraction that you ever saw?
- What is the farthest distance you ever biked?
- What is the farthest distance you ever walked?
- What is the weirdest thing you needed to buy while on vacation?
- What is your favorite candy?
- What is your favorite color car?
- What is your favorite family vacation?
- What is your favorite food?
- What is your favorite gas station drink or food?
- What is your favorite license plate design?
- What is your favorite restaurant?
- What is your favorite smell?
- What is your favorite song?
- What is your favorite sound that nature makes?
- What is your favorite thing to bring home from a vacation?
- What is your favorite vacation with friends?
- What is your favorite way to relax?

- Where is the farthest place you ever traveled in a car?
- Where is the farthest place you ever went North, South, East and West?
- Where is your favorite place in the world?
- Who is your favorite singer?
- Who taught you how to drive?
- Who will you miss the most while you are away?
- Who if the first person you will contact when you get to your destination?
- Who brought you on your first vacation?
- Who likes to travel the most in your life?
- Would you rather be hot or cold?
- Would you rather drive above, below, or at the speed limited?
- Would you rather drive on a highway or a back road?
- Would you rather go on a train or a boat?
- Would you rather go to the beach or the woods?

TRAVEL BUCKET LIST

1.

2.

3.

4.

5.

6.

7.

8.

9.

10.

NOTES